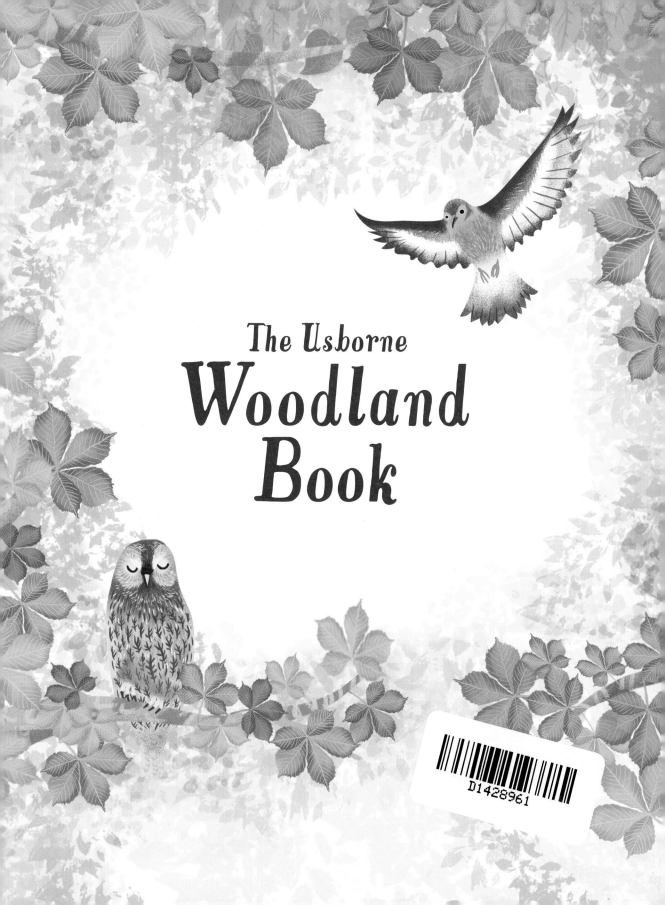

The Usborne
Woodland
Book

For links to websites where you can take
virtual tours of woodlands, watch video
clips of woodland wildlife and find out how
to identify leaves, trees, birds and other
animals, go to the Usborne Quicklinks
website at www.usborne.com/quicklinks and
enter the keywords 'woodland book'.

Please follow the safety guidelines at the
Usborne Quicklinks website.

The Usborne Woodland Book

Illustrated by Natalie Hughes

Written by Emily Bone and Alice James

Designed by Helen Edmonds,
Anna Gould and Zoe Wray

Woodland consultant: Laura McConnell
Wildlife expert: Zoë Simmons

Guide to the woodland book

You are here

Be introduced to a **WOODLAND** on pages 6-7.

Explore a **SUMMER WOODLAND** on pages 8-9.

Use your senses to **FEEL, SMELL AND LISTEN** to the woods on pages 10-11.

BE A WOODLAND BIRD WATCHER on pages 14-15.

On pages 12-13, discover **ALL SORTS OF LEAVES.**

Find out which **CREATURES** live in the woods on pages 16-21.

See what happens to the woods **AS SUMMER ENDS** on pages 22-25.

What are **ANCIENT WOODS?** Find out on pages 34-35.

Find out about **WOODLAND SHELTERS** on pages 26-27.

Discover mysterious **MUSHROOMS** on pages 28-29.

Learn about woodland creepy crawlies that live **UP HIGH** and **DOWN LOW** on pages 30-33.

All kinds of creatures make the woods their home – from squirrels and birds in the treetops to scuttling creepy crawlies in the undergrowth.

A woodland can be anything from a vast forest full of thousands of trees, to a little wooded area in your local park. Most woods are a mix of different types of trees, along with a tangle of other plants – shrubs, vines, ferns, flowers and mosses.

Many tales, myths and stories have been set in woods. Woods can feel dark and mysterious, or exciting and full of adventures. Step between the trees, look up at the tall branches, feel the cool, shady air and go exploring.

Ferns often carpet the ground, along with woodland wildflowers in the spring.

Some woodlands have trees
that are hundreds, maybe even
thousands, of years old.

This little symbol highlights
an important safety or
environmental warning.

If you do visit the woods, make sure you stay safe.
Carry water, a map and a fully charged phone and
never go anywhere without a responsible grown-up.
Don't pick any plants or flowers, and try to leave
everything as you found it, too.

In a summer woodland,

a canopy of leafy branches stretches out to create shade on the damp ground. Old trees soar high above scrubby bushes, twisting vines, young saplings, and delicate woodland flowers.

Look up and down and notice the different things around you.

The top of a tree is called its crown.

Look out for big birds, such as birds of prey, perching up here.

Leaves take in light, air and water to make food and help the tree grow.

Vines wind their way up, trying to get to the sunlight.

The strong, high branches of tall trees stretch up and out. The leaves angle themselves so they're bathed in sunlight.

Thick, gnarled bark protects the tree trunk and branches. One layer of wood grows inside the trunk each year, making the bark outside expand and crack.

Young trees, called saplings

A sturdy trunk supports the branches and takes water up to the leaves.

Frilly green plants, called ferns

Huge roots run deep into the ground. They keep the tree upright and suck up water and nutrients from the soil.

Mosses are plants that grow in thick clumps on damp ground.

Virginia creeper

Dogwood

Bushes and small trees grow well in the shade.

The shady woodland floor feels spongy underfoot because it's made up of layers of soft leaves, wood and dead plants. These rot down and create food for trees and other plants.

Woodland flowers grow in patches of sunlight.

Virginia waterleaf

Feel, smell and listen

to the woods. Close your eyes to let your other senses do the exploring.

Feel the bark on different tree trunks. What is the texture like?

Papery

Smooth

Squashy
moss

Scratchy
lichen

Ridged

Sticky
sap

Oniony
wild garlic

Smell the woods around you by standing still and taking some deep breaths.

Can you tell what the weather's been like? Does it smell like wet plants or dry, dusty ground?

Woody
trunk

Earthy
mud

Dung

Fragrant
wildflowers

Plink

Rain falling on
leaves and dripping
on the ground

Plink

Tap
Tap
Tap

Whoosh

Chirp,
chirp

Baby birds
in a nest

A woodpecker
searching for
insects

Bzzz

Flap

Listen: what can you hear? Some animals,
such as deer, have big ears so they can hear
things from far away. Cup your hands around
your ears to make your own deer ears.

Scratch

Scrambling
squirrel

Thud
Thud

Squelch

Falling
pine cone

Bzzz

Thump

Bees, wasps and
flies visiting
flowers

All sorts of leaves

grow in woodlands. The leaves of some trees, called deciduous trees, turn yellow or red in autumn, and drop to the floor. Other trees, called evergreens, keep leaves on their branches all year. Here are some common leaf shapes, and the types of trees you'll find them on.

Oval leaves

- Beech
- Poplar
- Aspen
- Birch
- Hazel
- Elm

Birch leaves have a jagged outline.

Aspen leaves go bright yellow in autumn.

Beech leaves have a smooth outline.

Veins carry water and food through the leaves.

Wavy-edged leaves

- Oak
- Hawthorn

Each wave is called a lobe.

Spiky-edged leaves

- Holly

Needles

- Pine
- Larch
- Fir

Trees with needles are evergreen. Evergreen leaves are usually green, tough and glossy, to protect the veins inside from the winter cold.

Hand-shaped leaves

- Horse chestnut
- Sycamore
- Maple

Horse chestnut leaves have five sections known as 'fingers'.

Maple leaves turn a vivid red before they fall.

Lots of leaves on one stem

- Elder
- Ash

Ash leaves fall when they are still green – they don't turn red or orange beforehand.

Little leaves on one stem like this are known as leaflets.

Soft fan-like fronds

- Cedar
- Sequoia
- Cypress

For help identifying leaves go to the **Usborne Quicklinks** website (see front of book).

Be a woodland bird watcher

and learn how to spot birds hidden in leafy, shady trees.
Sit quietly and *look up* for these different birds.
You could close your eyes and *listen*, too.

Notice little birds flitting from branch
to branch, or hanging upside down picking
off bugs, seeds and berries. These are
probably finches and tits.

American
goldfinches

Whistle, pew, whistle

Blackbird

Long-tailed tits

Tsee, tsee

Some birds will chatter in groups,
while others will stand on their own
and give a long, trilling call.

Fee-bee   Chickadees

Chaffinch

Pink, pink, pink

You'd never see all these
birds in one place. To identify
which bird you've spotted,
you need to look closely at
its markings and size, and
listen to its call, too.

Crow

Caw, caw

Tawny owl

Peer up above the treetops. You might spot crows or birds of prey, such as buzzards and sparrowhawks, soaring in the sky.

Owls are awake at night, but in the day some will sit on shady branches, close to tree trunks.

In spring, try to find a bird flying to and from one spot. It might have a nest full of hungry chicks there.

Nuthatch

Jay's nest

Cheep, cheep

All kinds of birds root around in leaves seeking out tasty grubs, nuts and seeds on the woodland floor.

Woodpeckers, treecreepers and nuthatches hop up, down and around tree trunks, looking for bugs to eat.

Woodpeckers

Jay

Pigeon

Woodland creatures are more likely to hide in or behind trees than be out in the open.

Woodmouse

Hare

Deer

Boar

Sit or stand very still so you can **search silently** for creatures. If you don't move or make much noise some animals might make an appearance.

z z z z z z

Bears sleep in hollows under big trees.

Snake

Snakes and lizards need heat from the sun to move. So look for them basking in open clearings.

Lizard

Worm

Caterpillar

Lots of creepy crawlies live in the undergrowth.

Spider

Beetle

Birds and squirrels build nests out of sticks and moss among the branches.

Look up among the branches for birds, insects and squirrels. They might be flying or scampering around, or resting on twigs and leaves.

Owls and bats sleep in trees. Look out for holes and hollows where they might be resting.

Beaver lodge

Some animals make their homes in or near woodland rivers.

Pine marten

Stoat

Badger sett

Rabbit

Rabbit warren

Vole

Explore the floor for holes dug into the mud. Lots of woodland creatures live in burrows underground.

Cicada

You won't see all these animals in the same place – they live in different woodlands around the world. To find out about many of these animals, go to the **Usborne Quicklinks** website (see front of book).

Chipmunk burrow

Footprints

can give a clue to the creatures that might be nearby. Following the trails left by animals is called tracking. The clearest tracks are left in mud where the ground is soft, so search for footprints in a muddy woodland.

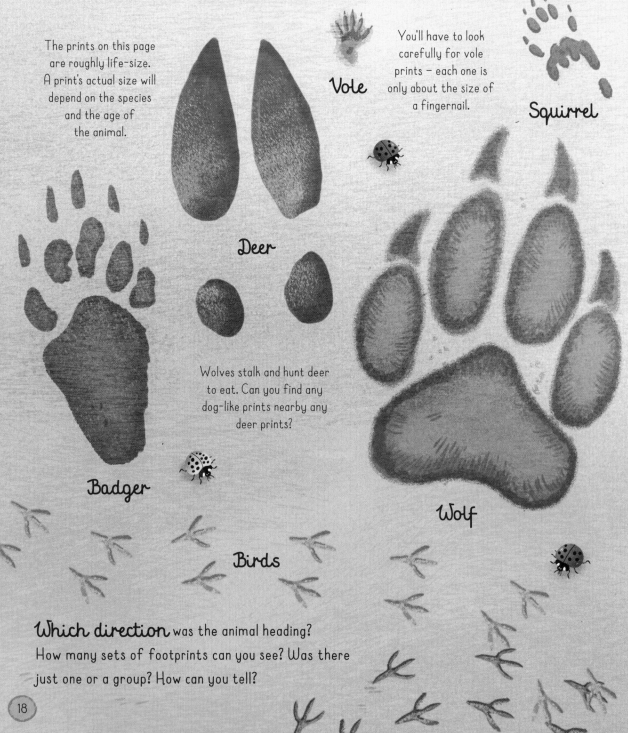

The prints on this page are roughly life-size. A print's actual size will depend on the species and the age of the animal.

Vole

You'll have to look carefully for vole prints – each one is only about the size of a fingernail.

Squirrel

Deer

Wolves stalk and hunt deer to eat. Can you find any dog-like prints nearby any deer prints?

Badger

Wolf

Birds

Which direction was the animal heading?
How many sets of footprints can you see? Was there just one or a group? How can you tell?

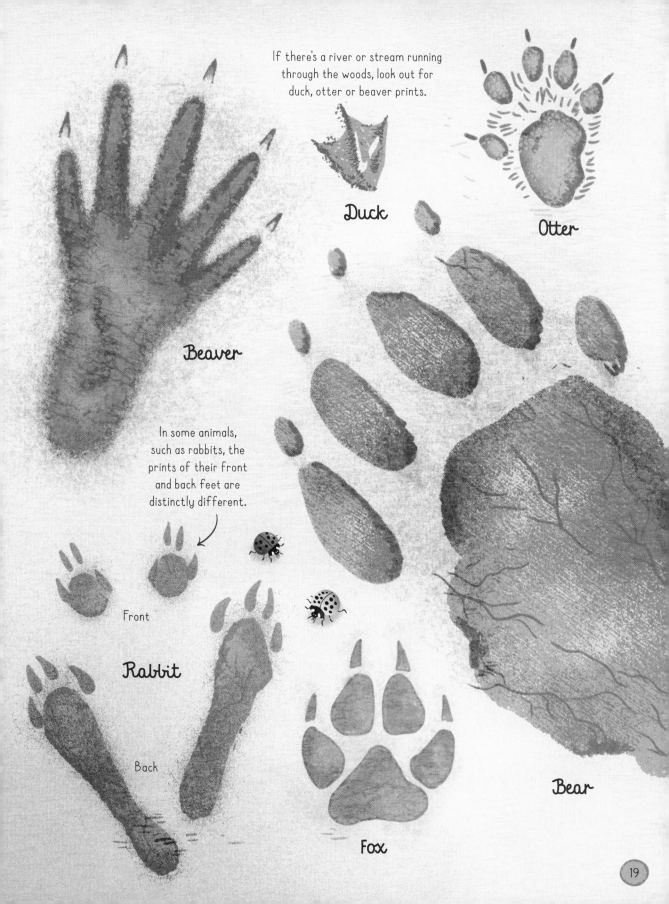

Beaver

If there's a river or stream running through the woods, look out for duck, otter or beaver prints.

Duck

Otter

In some animals, such as rabbits, the prints of their front and back feet are distinctly different.

Front

Rabbit

Back

Fox

Bear

Woodland animals leave lots of clues, including droppings, hair, and marks on trees, as well as footprints.

Broken eggshells, fallen from nests where chicks have hatched

Nuts cracked open by a bird's beak

Mice, voles and squirrels eat nuts too.

Droppings below a nest

Here are some signs that a **bird** has been around...

Feathers on the ground or caught on branches

Tooth marks on mushrooms

A bare patch of ground where a deer has rolled around in the mud

Black, shiny dung, pointed at one end

These are the clues a **deer** might leave...

Bark rubbed away by antlers

20

Long dark hairs, caught on brambles or fences

Path dug under a bush or tree

Sloppy piles of dung, in holes in the ground

Claw scratch marks on fallen logs

Clues that a **badger** has been nearby...

Badgers often leave all their dung together outside their setts.

Low twigs that have been munched

Tufts of pale fur caught on a fence

Signs left by a **rabbit**...

Small grassy pellets of dung

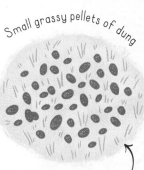

Warrens dug in the ground near the base of trees

Scientists call dung they use for identification scat.

You might see wild apples, pears, cherries or damsons growing.

How many falling leaves can you catch?

As summer ends, the weather gets cooler and the woods begin to change again. Ripe fruits, nuts and seeds drop to the ground for hungry woodland animals to eat. Leaves start to turn red, orange and yellow, and gradually flutter off the trees.

Birds, deer and wild boar munch on fallen nuts and fruit.

Squirrels and jays collect nuts and bury them in the ground for winter.

Some vines and shrubs grow bright berries.

Wild mushrooms grow in the undergrowth. Find out more on pages 28-29.

Fallen leaves turn crunchy, then rot down into squelchy leaf litter.

Go on an autumn walk to look for signs of the new season.
See if you can spot some of the things below...

Soft fruit

Damson

Elderberries

Bright purple or black berries

Shiny nut

Acorn

A **leaf** that's still half-green

Spiky seed or nut case

Wild apple

Pine cone - seed case from a conifer tree

Sweet chestnut

Bright red berries

Seeds from maples or sycamores are known as **keys** or **helicopters**.

Rosehip

An **orange, yellow, red** or **brown leaf**

A tree's seeds come in all sorts of shapes and sizes, and some have protective cases. A seed contains the ingredients for a brand new tree. Seeds drop to the ground late in the year, and some eventually grow into new trees.

Nuts are tough cases that protect a precious seed inside.

Oak

Oak nuts are called acorns.

Beech

Beechnut

Squirrels bury acorns to eat in the winter. They often forget them, and the acorns are left to grow into new oaks.

Pine

Hazel

Hazelnuts drop to the floor, and some get eaten by birds.

Pine trees grow cones full of seeds late in summer.

When the cones open up, seeds are blown away by the wind, and scatter widely on the ground.

Some trees grow **fruits** around their seeds, to attract animals to eat them. After animals digest the fruit, the seeds end up on the woodland floor and start to grow.

Crab apple

Crab apple

Blackthorn

Sloe

Blackthorn fruits are called sloes. The seed in a sloe is inside a hard case called a stone.

Berries are small fruits with tiny seeds inside.

Maple

Maple seeds, called keys, or helicopters, spiral down to the ground in the wind.

Rowan

Clusters of bright red berries

European sycamores have these floating seeds as well.

Helicopter

25

Woodland shelters

used to be built by forest dwellers
to sleep in, rest in or keep dry
in a storm.

Tree teepees have branches propped
in a circle, around a tree trunk.

Teepees can provide cool
shade when it's hot outside,
and some shelter from the
wind when it's cold.

The sticks need
to be tall enough
for a person to
fit inside.

The ground inside
is cleared to make
it more comfy.

Stick shelters are built around a main branch wedged between two trees.

Sticks are propped against the main branch, along both sides.

Leaf huts can be warm and waterproof.

Sides are packed with leaves, ferns and twigs.

A backpack can be used to close up the entrance and keep out the cold.

Leaf huts are a triangular shape. They're widest at the entrance and narrowest at the back. So a person can fit in lying down, with their head at the front.

Mushrooms

Mushrooms pop up in woods in spring and late summer. They are the fruits of underground living things called fungi. All kinds of wonderfully named varieties grow on the shady woodland floor, on soggy rotten wood and damp tree trunks.

Only ever look at mushrooms and never touch or pick them. Some are very poisonous and will make you seriously ill, or even kill you.

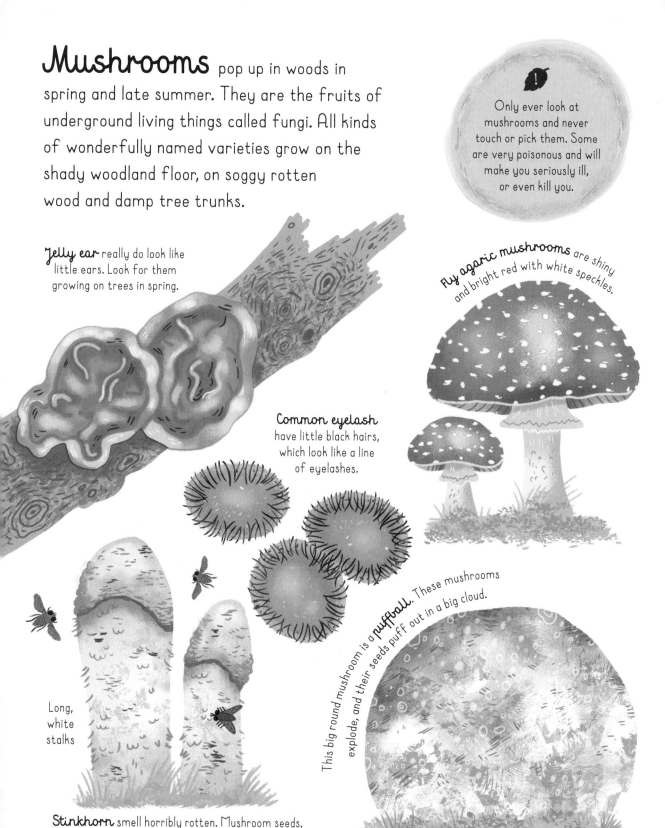

Jelly ear really do look like little ears. Look for them growing on trees in spring.

Fly agaric mushrooms are shiny and bright red with white speckles.

Common eyelash have little black hairs, which look like a line of eyelashes.

Long, white stalks

This big round mushroom is a **puffball**. These mushrooms explode, and their seeds puff out in a big cloud.

Stinkhorn smell horribly rotten. Mushroom seeds, called spores, are tiny. The smell attracts flies, which then help to spread the spores on their feet.

Candlesnuff or **stag's horn fungus** has lots of spiky prongs.

Amethyst deceivers start off bright purple and turn pale as they grow bigger.

Honey fungus feeds on tree roots.

Look for mushrooms growing in big circles, known as **fairy rings**.

People used to think these were made by dancing fairies. Stepping inside brings bad luck, unless you run around the ring 9 times first.

← Shaggy parasol

Dead man's fingers look like hands poking out of the ground.

Witches' butter grows as bright yellow squiggly patches on trees.

Up high in the woods in late spring or summer, there will be hundreds of different bugs flying, hopping and crawling in the trees.

Butterflies, bees, wasps and flies go from flower to flower. They're feeding on a sweet liquid inside, called nectar.

Butterflies perch in sunny spots, basking in the warm sun.

Brimstone butterfly

Hoverfly

Honey bees turn nectar into honey inside their tummies.

Speckled wood butterfly

Bumblebee

Wild cherry

Shield bugs squeeze out a nasty-smelling liquid if they're threatened.

Tussock moth caterpillar

Caterpillars gobble up lots of leaves.

Tree wasps scrape wood from trees. They chew up the wood in their mouths, then spit it out to build nests.

Look for sticky, silky spider webs catching the sunlight.

Garden spider

You might see a wasp's nest hanging from a tree branch.

Cricket

Crickets and grasshoppers make a chirping sound by rubbing their legs or wings together.

If you shake a branch you can take a closer look at bugs living there. You could put a few white sheets of paper under a tree or low-hanging branch. Gently shake the tree, wait for 5-10 seconds, and a few bugs should fall on the paper. Remember, never touch the bugs, and leave them alone to go back to their homes.

Chirp, chirp

Chirp, chirp

Down low on the leafy woodland floor, bugs and other creatures scuttle, slither, hop or burrow in and under crumbly rotting wood. Find a stick and carefully lift up a fallen branch or log to look underneath. Remember to put the log back in its place again.

Stag beetles have huge antlers. You might see them fighting other beetles.

Wolf spiders race after their prey to catch them.

Some woodlice roll up into a ball to protect themselves.

Earwigs have fierce-looking pincers that they use to fight off other bugs.

Tiny wood-boring beetles burrow into damp logs and make lots of holes, like these.

Watch for wiggly worms. They eat decomposing roots and leaves.

Frogs love to hide in damp places. Look out for little baby ones in early summer.

Different types of snails have different markings on their shells.

Banded snail

Millipedes have lots and lots of legs.

Shelf fungus

Mushrooms grow on fallen trees.

Slugs like damp places. They make slimy trails behind them as they move.

Beetle grubs burrow into wood, gobbling it up as they move.

Snakes slither under fallen trees to rest or hide. If you do spot a snake it's best to leave it alone or it might bite you.

Ants forage for food on the woodland floor.

Some woods are ancient – they've been growing in the same place for hundreds of years. Look out for interesting, characterful trees and signs that people have lived in the woods.

Ancient woods are usually a higgledy-piggledy mix of different trees, with lots of other plants growing around them.

Woodland wildflowers prefer ground that hasn't been disturbed for a long time, so they're more likely to grow in ancient woods.

Look for signs of past forest-dwellers, such as a clearing, walls, mounds, pits or anything else that seems out of place.

Trees with lots of thin trunks are called coppices. Years ago, they were cut down to stumps, which made them grow like this. Then, they were cut down again to be used as fence posts.

Ancient trees

are gnarled, bumpy and often crooked. The bark has lots of splits, hollows and holes. Imagine what kind of a life the tree has had, and all the things it's seen.

Up in the branches

you might see jagged breaks where parts of an old tree have died and broken off.

Mushrooms, mosses and liverworts – unusual flat, green plants – like to live on and around old trees.

Look out for animals nesting in holes and creepy crawlies darting in and out of the bark, eating old, rotting wood.

Hug a tree to get a rough idea of how old it is.

If you and a friend can put your arms around a trunk and not touch fingers, the tree might be over 100 years old.

An oak that has a trunk two hugs wide is roughly 150 years old.

Explore the woods while you're on a walk,
by collecting interesting things or making a picture map.

Make a memory twig.
Go on a short walk and collect things that will remind you about what you've seen and the route you've taken. Tie each one to a twig as you walk along, starting from the bottom and going up the twig.

!
Never go out walking in the woods unless you have a grown-up with you. It's safest to carry a map, too.

!
Never pick any living plant, and scatter any objects you've collected before you leave.

Pine branch

Pebble

Birch leaves

Bird's feather

Oak leaves

Fern

Moss

Cedar branch

Pine cone

Beech leaves

Beechnut

Acorn

Birch bark

Make a picture map inspired by what you've seen on a woodland walk. Add different trees, landmarks, hilly areas and anything else you think is interesting.

Wild woods

Starting point

Camp site

Badger sett

Mark which way you think is north.

Lake

Big oak

Bird's nest

Great view from here!!

Include a key to explain the different things on your map:

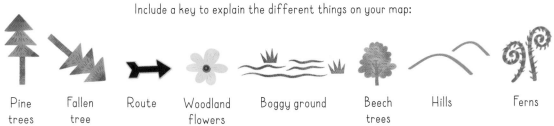

Pine trees

Fallen tree

Route

Woodland flowers

Boggy ground

Beech trees

Hills

Ferns

Write a woodland journal.

If you're camping in the woods (or staying nearby), it's a chance to get up early and spend the whole day from sunrise to sunset being super-observant. Make a sketch or note of the things you see, hear and smell. You could write more next time you go to the woods.

BLUEBELL FOREST CAMPING TRIP

DAY 1:
MORNING

The sun rose at 6:30 this morning.
Birds singing very loudly.

ANIMALS I SPOTTED THIS MORNING

4 rabbits

1 deer (wow!)

Birds hopping around in tree branches.

Spider weaving a web - very pretty!

Very exciting! Saw a ring of mushrooms!

What time does the sun rise?

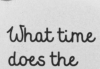

Very early after the sun rises, listen to the birds singing.

Can you hear the same call over and over again?
Or a mixture of different ones?
Which birds do you see first?
What are they doing?

Early in the morning, look out for rabbits and deer, nibbling on grass and plants. Do you see any other animals?

Early morning water droplets on grass, or glistening on trees and spider webs, is called dew. It's made by the cool night air meeting the warming morning sun.

Take a note of what you see on a walk.

If you can see the sky through the trees, do you notice any clouds? What are they like?

These dark clouds could mean rain is on the way.

What times of day do you see most birds and insects?

How many plants and trees can you identify?

Do plants or trees change throughout the day? Do some droop in the heat, or sway more in the wind?

AFTERNOON:

At 3pm black clouds through the trees followed by a shower of rain. Couldn't see many insects or birds. After the rain stopped, saw lots of bees and flies.

EVENING:

Sunset at 8:30pm. Twit-twoo noises - owls? Back at the campsite we watched bats swooping overhead, told stories and sang songs.

Sheltered under an oak tree.

When does the sun set each day,

and when does it start to get dark?

As the sun sets, birds are getting ready to sleep. You might see crows circling and calling.

Can you see any night animals waking up, such as bats and owls?

Silhouettes and shadows

appear as dusk draws in, and the setting sun streams through the trees.

You could tell stories as the sun sets. All kinds of tales, from ghost stories to fairy tales, use the woods as a setting. Tell a story using one of these starters:

It was a still, warm night. They could hear different creatures rustling, snuffling and hooting among the dark trees...

She dashed through the forest, dodging trees and ducking under branches...

He knelt to the floor and looked at the footprints. "What type of animal came through here?" he wondered aloud...

See page 52-53 for more woodland story-telling.

The evening sky can give you clues about tomorrow's weather.

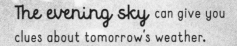
"A ring around the moon, rain's coming soon"

"Red sky at night, shepherd's delight"

Sayings like this are known as weatherlore. A red or pink evening sky means tomorrow's weather will be dry. Shepherds and sailors watch the sky closely, to know how they'll be affected by the weather.

Look for frosty, pale rings around the evening moon – it means there's moisture in the air, and rain could be on its way.

You could send **light messages** in the dark, by turning a lamp on and off.

Try coming up with a few signals to send to your friends or family.

Long flash = Meet you outside!

2 short flashes = Shh, I can hear an animal.

At night the woods come alive with a new set of creatures – ones that sleep during the day and are awake at night, known as nocturnal creatures. This is the twilight world of bats, moths, and twinkling fireflies.

Fluttering moths

Noisy crickets and grasshoppers

Chirp, chirp

If you trek through the woods as it gets dark, you might hear and see these nocturnal animals. (But never go out at night without a grown-up.)

Beetles

Ants

Snuffling badgers

Foraging mice

Through the canopy, stars twinkle high in the sky. Stars are most visible on clear nights, in places without any streetlights.

Bats

Owls swoop through the trees. Listen out for a screech, or a gentle twit-twoo.

Fireflies are a kind of beetle. Their bodies give off a bright pinprick of light to attract mates.

Twit - twoo

Fireflies

Lots of creatures are attracted to light. If you leave a light on the ground for a few minutes, insects will often gather around it.

Bright, glowing animal eyes

Fox

Old thrush's nest

The bare branches expose old nests made by birds and squirrels.

A winter woodland on a cold, frosty day,

can look bare and empty. But, even in the depths of winter, the woods are alive with different plants, and animals seeking food. Here are some things to look out for...

Sticky white berries

Mistletoe is a plant that grows in messy balls in the tops of trees.

Fragile leaf skeletons are made when the soft parts of leaves have crumbled away to reveal the stems and tiny veins running through them.

Conifer

Evergreen plants keep their leaves through the winter. They stand out clearly in the woods.

Old bracket fungus on tree trunks

Holly has spiky leaves and bright red berries.

Animals will venture further in search of food in winter so you're more likely to see them.

If there's snow or frost, look out for animal footprints.

Waxwings

Flocks of birds feed on berries that grew in late summer.

Rowan berries

When it's really cold, spiky icicles may form as water droplets freeze on tree branches.

Ivy grows berries which birds love to eat.

Witches' brooms are masses of shoots growing out from tree branches. This happens when the tree is damaged or has a disease.

When a tree's leaves have fallen in winter, look at the shade and texture of the **bark** around its wooden trunk.

Here are some of the most common types of bark and where to find them.

Smooth or gently bumpy

- Beech
- Rowan
- Holly

Beech bark

Spotted bark that looks like **scales**

- Oak
- Maple
- Spruce
- Hawthorn

Bumpy and dotted with holes

- Poplar
- Hazel

Poplar bark

Beech trees often have pieces of bark missing – squirrels use strips of the smooth bark in their nests.

This is the bark of an oak tree. It gets more knobbly, gnarled and knotted over time.

For more tips on identifying trees, go to the *Usborne Quicklinks* website (see front of book).

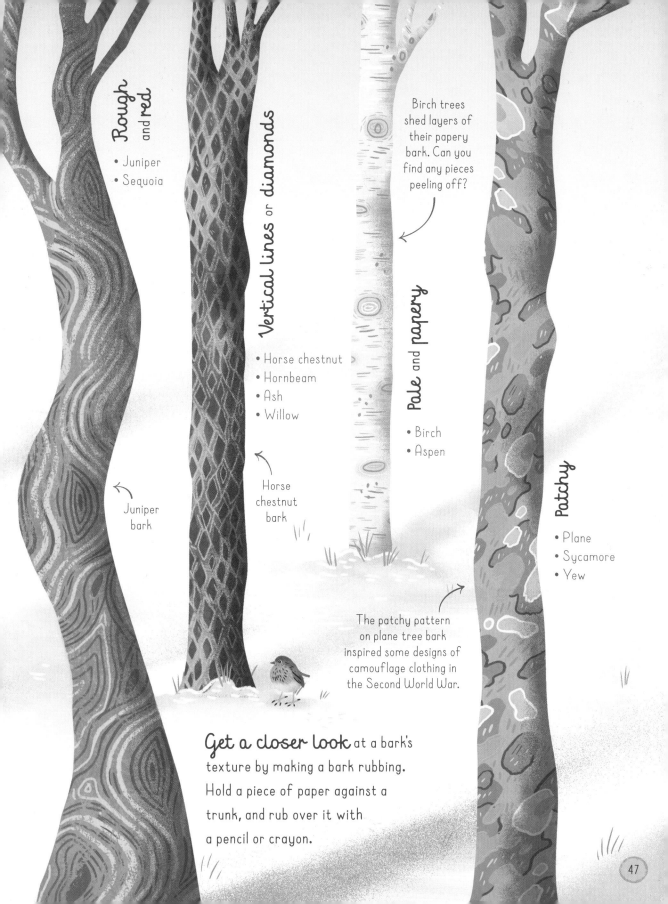

Rough and **red**
- Juniper
- Sequoia

Vertical lines or **diamonds**
- Horse chestnut
- Hornbeam
- Ash
- Willow

Horse chestnut bark

Juniper bark

Birch trees shed layers of their papery bark. Can you find any pieces peeling off?

Pale and **papery**
- Birch
- Aspen

Patchy
- Plane
- Sycamore
- Yew

The patchy pattern on plane tree bark inspired some designs of camouflage clothing in the Second World War.

Get a closer look at a bark's texture by making a bark rubbing. Hold a piece of paper against a trunk, and rub over it with a pencil or crayon.

Explorers navigate

through woods using all sorts of techniques. Finding their way and not getting lost often relies on being able to work out which direction they're facing – north, south, east or west.

The **stars** have helped people navigate for centuries.

In the Northern Hemisphere, the North Star shines over the North Pole.

In the Southern Hemisphere, the Southern Cross (Crux) points south.

Explorers also make note of any landmarks, or features of the landscape, such as a river. They can match these to a map, or follow them to find their way back.

Trees

A hut or cabin

A clearing with no trees

A river or stream

Sun and shade influence the way things grow, which gives clues too. In the Northern Hemisphere, it's sunnier on the south side, and shadier on the north side.

The sun rises in the east, and sets in the west, everywhere in the world.

The side of a tree that gets most sun usually grows best. Look out for asymmetric trees – the biggest side probably points south.

Leaves on the shady north side tend to be larger and darker than on the south side. They are bigger to get enough sunlight to make energy.

Moss grows best in moist places. It's usually damper and darker on the north side of trees, where there's less sun.

In the Southern Hemisphere, these will be flipped – the north side is brighter and the south side is darker.

Find your way using just a stick and a couple of stones.

Push a long stick upright into the ground on a sunny day, and put a stone at the end of its shadow. Wait 15 minutes, then put another stone at the end of its shadow, which will have moved. Draw an imaginary line between the two stones. Following that line, the first stone points west and the second stone points east.

E

Stone 2

Stone 1

W

Wild cherry blossom

Springtime!

At the end of winter, warm sunlight streams into the woods. Bare branches burst into life again. New buds, woodland flowers and shoots appear, along with busy birds, and the first bees and butterflies.

Look out for bees or butterflies feeding from flowers.

Crab apple blossom

Swallowtail butterfly

Fruit trees grow little buds, which open into white and pink blossom.

Delicate, deep-blue, bell-shaped flowers

Lesser celandines have bright-yellow star-shaped flowers.

Thousands of bluebells can grow in one area, creating a stunning sea of blue.

If these flowers close their petals, it could mean rain is on the way.

Fluffy, dangling flowers, called catkins, grow on some trees, including hazel and willow.

The word catkin comes from the Dutch for kitten, 'katteken', because they look like kittens' tails.

Hazel catkins

Birds hop and fly around collecting twigs, moss and other things to make their nests.

Budbursts are buds that have just opened into brand new leaves.

Blue tit

Wild garlic has spiky white flowers.

Elder budburst

Ferns are frondy woodland plants that die in winter and grow again in spring.

Trilliums have three leaves and bright white flowers with three petals.

Their spiral-shaped leaves slowly uncurl as they grow.

You'll probably smell the oniony scent of wild garlic before you see it!

Tales and legends are often set in woods,

because they can seem like mysterious places where people get lost, things lurk in the darkness, and magic happens...

Lots of **fairy tales** take place in woods.

Rapunzel was locked away in a tall tower, deep in the heart of the woods...

You could try writing your own story set in the woods. Are the woods threatening and dark, or peaceful and full of kind, woodland creatures?

Little Red Riding Hood walked through the woods to visit her grandmother...

Hansel and Gretel scattered breadcrumbs through the woods...

Light-carrying creatures appear in woodland stories from all over the world.

The characters carry misty lights that lead people off safe paths. These cunning creatures have all sorts of names.

Will o' the wisp

Scientists think these eerie lights might actually be from real creatures that light up – fireflies, glow-worms, or the flash of an owl's white feathers.

Min min light

Pixie light

Fairy fire

Hinkypunk

Chir batti

For hundreds of years, all around the world, people have told **myths and folk tales** full of magic, mighty trees.

In Viking mythology, a great ash tree called Yggdrasil reached to the sky, and linked the Viking world together.

Look around at trunks to see if you can find bumps, knobs and knots that look like faces. How do they look? Sleepy, wise, angry?

Druids, religious leaders of ancient European people called the Celts, named themselves after 'druir' – an oak tree.

Oak trees live so long that in many myths and folk tales they are considered powerful and wise. They live about 50 years before they even start producing acorns.

Zeus, king of the Ancient Greek gods, and Jupiter, king of the Ancient Roman gods, were thought to control the sky and storms. They were both associated with oak trees, too. Scientists have discovered that oak trees are more likely to be struck by lightning than any other tree.

Trees, trees, as far as the eye can see...

Woodlands are full of different trees, from huge spreading oaks to thin wispy birches and tall spiky pines. Here are some of the trees mentioned in this book.

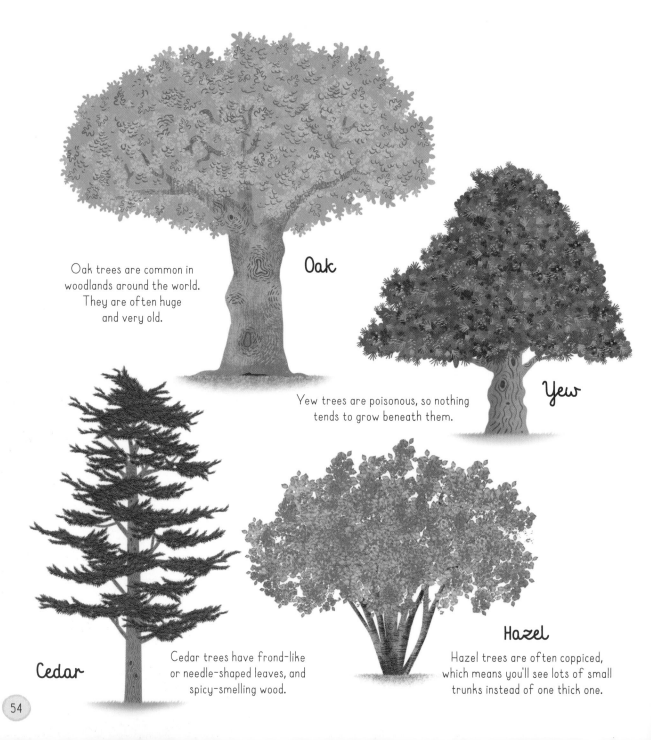

Oak

Oak trees are common in woodlands around the world. They are often huge and very old.

Yew

Yew trees are poisonous, so nothing tends to grow beneath them.

Cedar

Cedar trees have frond-like or needle-shaped leaves, and spicy-smelling wood.

Hazel

Hazel trees are often coppiced, which means you'll see lots of small trunks instead of one thick one.

Cherry trees bloom spectacularly, with clouds of pink and white blossom erupting all together. Leaves start to grow at the same time.

Blackthorn

The branches of blackthorn and cherry trees are laden with flowers in the spring, and fruits later in the year.

Horse chestnut

Cherry

Fir

Pine

Horse chestnut trees are easiest to identify by their leaves and seeds. They have leaves like five long fingers (see page 13) and prickly seed cases.

Fir, pine and spruce are all types of evergreen trees known as conifers. They have spiky needle-shaped leaves and wooden cones full of seeds.

European sycamore and maple trees are very common in woodlands. For more information about trees and how to identify them go to the *Usborne Quicklinks* website (see front of book).

Poplar

The leaves of most deciduous woodland trees turn yellow or orange late in the year, and then drop to the ground.

Maple

Beech

Aspen

Aspen and birch trees look very similar from a distance. They're both tall, with pale bark and green leaves that go yellow in autumn. Tell them apart by their leaves (see page 12).

Juniper

Sequoia

Some types of juniper grow into tall, twisted trees like this one, while others form bushes, covered in berries. Junipers have needle leaves, and strong-smelling bark.

Elder

Elder trees grow clusters of white flowers that birds and butterflies like to feed on.

Scot's pine

Holly

Sequoia trees, also known as giant redwoods, form huge, towering forests in America. They are the largest trees in the world.

57

Glossary

Here are some useful woodland words.

ancient woodland - woods that have been growing in the same place for hundreds of years.

bark - a tough layer covering a tree's trunk and branches to protect them. Bark looks different depending on the type of tree, so it's also used to help with identification.

blossom - flowers that grow on fruit trees, such as crab apple and cherry, in the spring.

bud - a little growth on a woodland plant that opens up into a leaf or flower.

canopy - the highest branches, which stretch out. In summer, canopies often block out the sunlight.

catkins - dangling flowers that grow on some trees, such as hazel and birch.

clearing - an open space in a woodland that was probably made when trees were cut down years ago to make space for grazing cattle or building homes.

compass - a tool with a little needle that points north. It's used for finding your way in the woods.

coppice - a tree, usually hazel or ash, that has been grown to have lots of thin trunks rather than one thick one. The trunks are cut down to make fences.

crown - the very top of a tree.

deciduous - a tree or plant that loses its leaves in the winter.

evergreen – a tree or plant that keeps its leaves through the winter. Leaves are usually thick and glossy, or pointy needles.

ferns – green plants with feathery, frondy leaves that grow on the woodland floor.

folklore – beliefs or stories relating to a particular place or thing, which have been passed down through generations.

frond – the feathery leaves of ferns and some evergreen trees, usually made up of lots of small leaves.

fruit – the fleshy surroundings some trees grow to contain their seeds. Animals eat fruit and spread the seeds in their droppings.

grub – a young insect, usually a beetle.

leaf skeleton – when all the softer parts of a fallen leaf break down in the winter and only the stem and veins are left behind.

lichen – a flat, crusty-feeling, greenish-yellow plant that grows on shady tree trunks and walls.

liverwort – a green plant that grows on trees. A liverwort has lots of small, flat green leaves.

moss – a small green plant that grows in damp places. It usually covers tree trunks and roots, damp ground and rocks in a woodland.

mushroom – the fruits of underground living things. Mushrooms grow above ground in spring or from late summer. There are lots of different varieties.

nectar – a sweet liquid inside flowers. Bees, butterflies and other insects feed on nectar.

nocturnal – animals that are awake at night and sleep during the day.

nut – a seed with a hard case that grows from flowers on some trees. If nuts are buried in the ground, they will grow into new trees.

pine cone – the fruit of a pine tree. Seeds called pine nuts grow inside them.

pollen – a dusty yellow powder inside flowers. When pollen is spread from one flower to another, it makes the plant or tree grow new seeds, nuts or fruits.

roots – the part of a tree that stretches down into the ground to hold it upright and suck up water and food from the soil.

sapling – a young tree.

scat – animal droppings.

seed – what a plant produces to grow new plants. Seeds grow from flowers, and are sometimes inside fruits or hard cases, called nuts.

sett – a badger's underground home.

tracking – looking for signs of where an animal has been in a wood.

trunk – thick, sturdy part of a tree which holds up the branches and takes water up to them.

veins – little tubes that run through each leaf of a plant or tree carrying water and food.

warren – the underground home of rabbits.

wildflowers – spring or summer flowers that grow on the woodland floor, usually in areas where sunlight streams in through the trees.

witches' brooms – lots of twigs sprouting out of branches on a tree. This usually happens because the tree has a disease.

Index

Managing Designer: Zoe Wray

Edited by Jane Chisholm

Digital manipulation by John Russell

First published in 2018 by Usborne Publishing Ltd., Usborne House,
83-85 Saffron Hill, London EC1N 8RT, England.
www.usborne.com Copyright © 2018 Usborne Publishing Ltd.